INTRODUCTION TO AI

Transform Your Business

Strategies, Applications and the
Future of AI for Entrepreneurs

KOUADIO KONAN JOEL

Copyright © 2024 KOUADIO KONAN JOEL

All rights reserved

The characters and events portrayed in this book are fictitious. Any similarity to real persons, living or dead, is coincidental and not intended by the author.

No part of this book may be reproduced, or stored in a retrieval system, or transmitted in any form or by any means, electronic, mechanical, photocopying, recording, or otherwise, without express written permission of the publisher.

Cover design by: Art Painter
Library of Congress Control Number: 2018675309
Printed in the United States of America

CONTENTS

Title Page
Copyright
Introduction to AI   1
BOOK OUTLINE   2
Foreword   8
Introduction   11
Part 1: Introduction to Artificial Intelligence for Business   12
Chapter 1: What is Artificial Intelligence?   13
Chapter 2: Why is AI Crucial for Modern Business?   23
Chapter 3: The Different Types of Artificial Intelligence   33
Chapter 4: Understanding AI Algorithms   41
Part 2: Integrating AI into Business Operations   50
Chapter 1: Development and Implementation of AI Solutions   51
Chapter 2: Business Process Automation   59
Chapter 3: Data Management and AI   67
Chapter 4: Security and AI   74
Chapter 1: Improving Customer Service with AI   83
Chapter 2: Marketing and Sales Optimization   90
Chapter 3: AI in Human Resources Management   97
Chapter 4: Financial Management and AI   105

Part 4: Strategies and Future of AI in Business	113
Chapter 1: Developing an AI Strategy for Your Business	114
Chapter 2: Ethics and Regulation of AI	122
Chapter 3: Preparing Your Business for the Future of AI	131
Chapter 4: Case Studies and Future Perspectives	139
Conclusion	147
Lexicon	151

INTRODUCTION TO AI

Transform Your Business

Strategies, Applications and the Future of AI for Entrepreneurs

BOOK OUTLINE

Introduction

- Presentation of the book
- Importance of AI for businesses
- Objectives and structure of the book

Part 1: Introduction to Artificial Intelligence for Business

Chapter 1: What Is Artificial Intelligence?

1.1 Definition and Key Concepts of AI

1.2 History and Evolution of AI

1.3 AI Operating Principles

1.4 Concrete Examples of AI

Chapter 2: Why Is Ai Crucial For Modern Business?

2.1 Benefits of AI for Businesses

2.2 Case Studies: Success with AI

2.3 Impacts on Competitiveness

2.4 Barriers and Challenges to AI Adoption

Chapter 3: The Different Types Of Artificial Intelligence

3.1 Weak AI vs Strong AI

3.2 Supervised Learning

3.3 Unsupervised Learning

3.4 Reinforcement Learning

Chapter 4: Understanding Ai Algorithms

4.1 Neural Networks and Deep Learning

4.2 Classification Algorithms

4.3 Regression Algorithms

4.4 Optimization Algorithms

Part 2: Integrating AI into Business Operations

Chapter 1: Development And Implementation Of Ai Solutions

1.1 AI Needs Assessment

1.2 Choice of AI Tools and Technologies

1.3 Development of AI Models

1.4 Integration and Deployment

Chapter 2: Business Process Automation

2.1 Identification of Automable Processes

2.2 Automation of Repetitive Tasks

2.3 Optimization of Production and Logistics

2.4 Impact of Automation on Employment

Chapter 3: Data Management And Ai

3.1 Data Collection and Preparation

3.2 Data Quality and Bias Management

3.3 Data Storage and Security

3.4 Analysis and Interpretation of Data

Chapter 4: Security And Ai

4.1 Security Threats Related to AI

4.2 Security Strategies for AI Systems

4.3 Compliance and Regulations

4.4 Data Security and Confidentiality

Part 3: Practical Applications of AI for Business

Chapter 1: Improving Customer Service With

Ai

1.1 Chatbots and Virtual Assistants

1.2 Personalization of the Customer Experience

1.3 Complaints Management and Technical Support

1.4 Case Studies: Customer Service and AI

Chapter 2: Marketing And Sales Optimization

2.1 Predictive Analysis and Market Segmentation

2.2 Targeted Advertising and Product Recommendations

2.3 Optimization of Marketing Campaigns

2.4 Performance Monitoring and Analysis

Chapter 3: Ai In Human Resources Management

3.1 Recruitment and Selection of Talent

3.2 Employee Training and Development

3.3 Performance Management and Retention

3.4 Forecasting Labor Needs

Chapter 4: Financial Management And Ai

4.1 Financial Forecasting and Analysis

4.2 Fraud Detection

4.3 Optimization of Investments

4.4 Financial Risk Management

Part 4: Strategies and Future of AI in Business

Chapter 1: Developing An Ai Strategy For Your Business

1.1 Development of an AI Roadmap

1.2 Identification of Strategic Objectives

1.3 Measuring and Evaluating AI Success

1.4 Continuous Adaptation and Innovation

Chapter 2: Ethics And Regulation Of Ai

2.1 Ethical Considerations for Using AI

2.2 Transparency and Accountability

2.3 AI Regulations and Standards

2.4 Future Ethical Challenges

Chapter 3: Preparing Your Business For The Future Of Ai

3.1 Emerging Trends in AI

3.2 Impact of New Technologies on AI

3.3 Training and Skills Development in AI

3.4 Building a Culture of Innovation

Chapter 4: Case Studies And Future Perspectives

4.1 Case Studies of Innovative Companies in AI

4.2 Lessons Learned and Best Practices

4.3 Future Perspectives for AI in Business

4.4 Conclusions and Recommendations

Conclusion

- Summary of key points of the book

- Continued importance of AI for business

- Encouragement of innovation and adaptation

FOREWORD

Artificial intelligence (AI) is redefining the contours of innovation and competitiveness in the business world. What was once the stuff of science fiction is now a tangible reality, with practical applications in almost every sector of the economy. From product recommendations on e-commerce platforms to autonomous vehicles to computer-assisted medical diagnostics, AI is radically transforming the way businesses operate and interact with their customers.

Yet despite its immense potential, AI remains a complex and often misunderstood field. Many companies are hesitant to adopt these cutting-edge technologies due to confusion around their practical applications, technical challenges and ethical considerations. This is where this book finds its usefulness.

"Introduction to AI: Transform Your Business" aims to be an accessible and comprehensive guide for business leaders, managers, entrepreneurs and all those who wish to understand and exploit the power of AI. We designed this book to demystify artificial intelligence, providing clear explanations of key concepts, inspiring case studies, and practical strategies for integrating AI into business operations.

We start with an introduction to the basics of AI, explaining its different branches, its applications and how it works. We continue by exploring how companies can develop an effective AI strategy, assess needs and opportunities, and measure the success of their initiatives. Dedicated chapters also cover optimizing operations using AI, process automation, human resource management and data security.

Another crucial aspect covered in this book is the ethics and regulation of AI. We discuss ethical challenges, potential biases and current regulations to ensure responsible and transparent use of AI.

Finally, we examine emerging trends and future prospects for AI in business, highlighting the technologies that will shape the years to come and offering actionable recommendations to keep your business at the cutting edge. innovation.

AI is not just a passing technological fad; it represents a fundamental shift in how businesses can improve efficiency, innovate and create value. We hope this book will inspire you and provide you with the tools to embark on your own journey into the exciting world of artificial intelligence.

Welcome to the age of AI. It's time to transform your business.

INTRODUCTION

Artificial intelligence (AI) is transforming the business world at breakneck speed. This book aims to guide entrepreneurs and business leaders through the concepts, strategies and practical applications of AI. By understanding how to take advantage of this revolutionary technology, you can not only improve your operations, but also prepare your business for a future marked by innovation and competitiveness.

PART 1: INTRODUCTION TO ARTIFICIAL INTELLIGENCE FOR BUSINESS

CHAPTER 1: WHAT IS ARTIFICIAL INTELLIGENCE?

1.1 Definition And Key Concepts Of Ai

Artificial intelligence (AI) is a branch of computer science dedicated to creating machines capable of performing tasks that normally require human intelligence. These tasks include learning, reasoning, pattern recognition, and decision making. AI can be classified into two main categories: weak (or narrow) AI and strong (or general) AI.

Weak AI is designed to perform specific, limited tasks, such as voice recognition, product recommendation, or autonomous navigation. For example, virtual assistants like Siri and Alexa use natural language processing algorithms to understand and answer user questions. These systems are very successful in their specific domains, but they lack the flexibility and generality of human intelligence.

Strong AI, on the other hand, aims to possess

cognitive abilities comparable to humans. She would be able to understand, learn and apply her knowledge to a variety of tasks, without being limited to a specific area. Although strong AI remains largely theoretical and in development, it represents the ultimate goal of many AI researchers.

Key concepts in AI include machine learning algorithms, neural networks, deep learning, natural language processing, and expert systems. Machine learning algorithms allow machines to improve with experience, while neural networks and deep learning help process complex data and extract hierarchical features. Natural language processing (NLP) allows machines to understand and generate human language, facilitating human-machine interaction. Expert systems, on the other hand, use rules and heuristics to simulate human reasoning in specific domains.

1.2 History And Evolution Of Ai

The history of AI dates back to the 1950s, when early researchers began exploring the possibility of creating intelligent machines. The term "artificial intelligence" was coined by John McCarthy in 1956 at the Dartmouth Conference, a seminal event that brought together AI pioneers to discuss the concepts and goals of this new field.

In the 1960s and 1970s, the first AI systems were based on simple rules and heuristics. These systems, called expert systems, used knowledge bases to simulate human reasoning in specific fields, such as medicine or geology. However, these systems were limited by the computing power of the time and the complexity of the problems they were trying to solve. They also lacked flexibility and could not adapt to new situations or learn from experience.

In the 1980s, AI experienced a period of stagnation often referred to as the "AI winter." High expectations have not been realized, and lack of funding has hampered progress in the field. Researchers began to realize that approaches based on rules and heuristics were insufficient for creating truly intelligent systems.

The AI revival began in the 1990s with advances

in machine learning. Unlike expert systems, machine learning algorithms allow machines to learn from data, without being explicitly programmed for each task. This approach has led to significant advances in areas such as speech recognition, computer vision and robotics.

The rise of deep learning in the 2010s marked a new era for AI. Deep learning uses deep neural networks to learn hierarchical representations of data, allowing AI systems to process raw data like images, text or sounds. This technology has led to revolutionary advances in areas such as image recognition, machine translation and video games.

1.3 Ai Operating Principles

AI works primarily through algorithms, which are sets of rules and instructions that computers follow to solve problems or make decisions. Machine learning algorithms allow AI systems to learn from data, improving their performance over time without being explicitly programmed for each task.

Machine learning algorithms fall into three main categories: supervised learning, unsupervised learning, and reinforcement learning.

- Supervised Learning: In supervised learning, algorithms learn from labeled data. This means that each data input is associated with a correct output, and the algorithm learns to make predictions or classifications based on that data. For example, an image recognition algorithm can be trained with thousands of images of cats and dogs, where each image is labeled as "cat" or "dog". The algorithm uses these examples to learn the distinctive characteristics of cats and dogs and can then correctly classify new images.

- Unsupervised Learning: Unsupervised learning involves the analysis of unlabeled data. The algorithm tries to find patterns or relationships in the data without explicit instruction on what to look for. Common techniques include clustering and principal component analysis. Clustering is used to group similar data into clusters. For example, a business can use clustering to segment its customers into groups with similar purchasing behaviors. This segmentation can help personalize marketing campaigns and improve customer satisfaction. Principal component analysis (PCA) is a technique used to reduce the dimensionality of data while retaining the most important information.

- Reinforcement Learning: Reinforcement learning is a technique where an agent learns to make decisions by interacting with an environment. The agent receives rewards or punishments based on its actions and adjusts its strategy to maximize rewards in the long term. A classic example of reinforcement learning is training an agent to play a video game. The agent begins by taking random actions and receives rewards for successful actions, such as scoring points, and punishments for unsuccessful actions, such as losing a life. Over time, the agent learns to develop strategies to maximize its scores. Reinforcement learning is used in real-world applications such as recommendation systems, robotics, and autonomous vehicles. For example, self-driving cars use reinforcement learning to navigate roads and avoid obstacles, continually learning from the driving experience.

AI algorithms are often combined with other technologies to create more powerful intelligent systems. For example, deep neural networks are used for deep learning, allowing AI systems to process complex data and extract hierarchical features. Convolutional neural networks (CNN) are used for image recognition, while recurrent neural networks (RNN) are used for natural language processing. Natural language processing algorithms enable machines to understand and generate human language, thereby facilitating human-machine interaction. Expert systems use rules and heuristics to simulate human reasoning in specific domains.

1.4 Concrete Examples Of Ai

The applications of AI are numerous and varied. Common examples include virtual assistants like Siri and Alexa, which use natural language processing to understand and answer user questions. Virtual assistants are capable of handling varied tasks such as setting appointments, sending messages, reading news, and controlling smart home devices. These assistants use natural language processing algorithms to understand user queries and provide relevant responses.

Netflix and Amazon's recommendation systems use machine learning algorithms to suggest movies, series and products based on user preferences. These systems analyze users' purchasing and viewing behaviors to provide personalized recommendations. For example, Netflix uses collaborative filtering algorithms to recommend movies and series based on users' viewing preferences.

Tesla's autonomous vehicles use deep learning and computer vision to navigate roads and avoid obstacles. Self-driving cars are equipped with sensors, cameras and radars that collect real-time data about the environment. Deep learning algorithms analyze this data to make driving decisions, such as changing lanes, stopping at red lights, or avoiding pedestrians. Autonomous vehicles represent a major advance in the field of mobility and road safety.

In healthcare, AI is used to analyze medical

images and help diagnose diseases, predict treatment outcomes, and personalize patient care. For example, computer vision algorithms can analyze X-ray, CT, or MRI images to detect abnormalities such as tumors or fractures. AI systems can also predict treatment outcomes by analyzing patients' medical data, such as medical history, previous treatments, and genetic characteristics. These predictions allow doctors to personalize care and improve patient outcomes.

In finance, AI is used to detect fraud, optimize investment portfolios and automate trading processes. Fraud detection algorithms analyze transactions in real time to identify suspicious behavior and prevent fraud. Portfolio management systems use machine learning algorithms to assess risk and recommend investment strategies. Trading robots use AI to execute trades automatically based on market conditions, thereby optimizing investment performance.

In summary, artificial intelligence is a constantly evolving field that is transforming many industries. Key concepts in AI, such as machine learning algorithms, neural networks, and natural language processing, enable machines to understand and interact with the world in more sophisticated ways. The history of AI is marked by significant advances, from early rule-based systems to today's deep learning technologies. The operating principles of AI are based on algorithms that allow systems to learn from data and improve their performance over time. Finally, concrete applications of AI, such as virtual assistants, recommendation systems and autonomous vehicles, demonstrate the immense potential of this technology to improve our daily lives and revolutionize many sectors.

CHAPTER 2: WHY IS AI CRUCIAL FOR MODERN BUSINESS?

2.1 Benefits Of Ai For Businesses

Artificial intelligence (AI) offers many benefits to modern businesses, transforming the way they operate and interact with their customers. These benefits include increased efficiency, improved data-driven decision making, and the ability to deliver personalized and engaging customer experiences.

One of the main advantages of AI is its ability to process and analyze massive volumes of data much faster than humans. This capability allows businesses to uncover valuable insights in real time and make more informed decisions. For example, AI algorithms can analyze market trends, predict consumer behaviors, and identify growth opportunities. Using AI, businesses can anticipate their customers' needs, adapt their marketing strategies, and optimize their operations to meet demand more efficiently.

By automating repetitive tasks, AI allows employees to focus on higher value-added activities. For example, chatbots can handle common customer support requests, freeing up human agents to handle more complex issues. In manufacturing operations, AI-enabled robots can perform repetitive production tasks with unparalleled precision and speed, reducing errors and increasing efficiency.

AI also improves decision-making by providing in-depth data analysis and accurate predictions. AI systems can analyze complex data sets to identify patterns and correlations invisible to the human eye. These insights allow decision-makers to make decisions based on concrete facts rather than hunches. For example, machine learning algorithms can predict financial market trends, allowing businesses to make informed investment decisions and minimize risks.

Another major benefit of AI is its ability to personalize customer experiences. By analyzing user behavioral data, AI algorithms can recommend relevant products and services, increasing customer satisfaction and loyalty. E-commerce platforms, for example, use AI to personalize product recommendations based on customer preferences and purchasing behaviors. This personalization not only improves user experience but also increases conversion rates and sales.

2.2 Case Studies: Success With Ai

Many companies have successfully integrated AI into their operations, demonstrating the tangible benefits of this technology.

Amazon: Amazon uses AI algorithms to optimize its supply chains and personalize product recommendations. Using AI, Amazon can predict product demand, adjust inventory accordingly, and minimize delivery times. Amazon's recommendation systems analyze customer purchasing behaviors to suggest relevant products, thereby increasing sales and customer satisfaction. For example, when a customer buys a book, the algorithm recommends other similar books based on the reading preferences of customers with similar tastes.

IBM Watson: IBM Watson helps healthcare professionals diagnose and treat complex diseases by analyzing large sets of medical data. Watson can identify possible treatment options, evaluate their effectiveness, and recommend personalized protocols for patients. This use of AI improves patient care and reduces medical errors. For example, Watson can analyze thousands of medical documents and patient records to recommend specific treatments for complex conditions like cancer, providing doctors with information based on the latest medical research.

JPMorgan Chase: In banking, JPMorgan Chase is using AI to automate the review of financial contracts, a process that once took thousands of human hours. The AI algorithm, called COiN (Contract Intelligence), can analyze legal documents in seconds, reducing costs and increasing efficiency. COiN also helps reduce human errors by automatically identifying key contractual clauses and verifying their compliance with current regulations.

2.3 Impacts On Competitiveness

Integrating AI can give businesses a significant competitive advantage. Companies that adopt AI can improve their products and services faster than competitors, respond to customer needs more effectively, and explore new market opportunities.

Personalization of Offers: Businesses using AI can personalize their offers more precisely. For example, streaming platforms like Netflix and Spotify use AI to recommend content based on user preferences, thereby increasing customer engagement and loyalty. By analyzing users' viewing and listening behaviors, these platforms can offer content that matches individual tastes, creating a more immersive and satisfying user experience.

Rapid Innovation: AI helps businesses innovate faster by identifying emerging trends and predicting future market needs. This allows companies to develop new products and services before their competitors, thereby capturing a larger market share. For example, fashion companies use AI to analyze trends on social media and fashion blogs, thereby anticipating which styles and colors will be popular in upcoming seasons. This ability to predict trends allows companies to design and launch clothing collections that meet consumer expectations even before they become mainstream.

Operational Efficiency: AI also allows companies to optimize their internal operations. For example, logistics companies use AI algorithms to optimize delivery routes, thereby reducing transportation costs and improving efficiency. Algorithms can analyze real-time traffic data, weather conditions and delivery schedules to plan the most efficient journeys, minimizing delays and costs.

Sustainable Competitive Advantage: By adopting AI, businesses can create a sustainable competitive advantage by integrating this technology into their culture and processes. Companies that invest in AI and develop internal data and technology skills are better equipped to adapt to market changes and stay at the forefront of innovation. For example, technology companies like Google and Facebook have integrated AI into their product development processes, allowing them to quickly launch new features based on user data and insights.

2.4 Barriers And Challenges To Ai Adoption

Despite its benefits, AI adoption also comes with challenges. These include the need for high-quality data, the technical complexity of implementing AI solutions, and ethical and regulatory concerns. Businesses must be prepared to invest in the skills and technologies needed to overcome these obstacles.

Data Management: One of the main challenges is data management. AI algorithms require clean, complete and relevant data to work effectively. Collecting, storing and processing this data can be expensive and complex. Additionally, data must be secure to protect user privacy and comply with data protection regulations. Companies must establish robust data infrastructures and data governance processes to ensure data integrity and quality.

AI Talent Shortage: Another challenge is the AI talent shortage. Companies need to recruit or train AI experts who can develop and deploy AI solutions. This can represent a significant investment of time and resources. Companies also need to ensure their employees have the skills needed to work with AI technologies, which may require continuing education programs and partnerships with educational institutions.

Technical Complexity: Implementing AI solutions can be technically complex, requiring in-depth knowledge of data science, software development, and technology project management. Businesses must be prepared to invest in modern technology infrastructure, such as cloud computing platforms and machine learning tools, to facilitate the development and deployment of AI solutions.

Ethical and Regulatory Considerations: Ethical and regulatory considerations are crucial. Companies must ensure their AI systems are transparent, fair and accountable. They must also comply with applicable laws and regulations to avoid sanctions and damage to their reputation. For example, data protection regulations like GDPR in Europe impose strict requirements on the collection, storage and processing of personal data. Companies must also address ethical issues, such as algorithmic bias and transparency of decisions made by AI, to ensure that their AI systems are used fairly and responsibly.

Acceptance and Adoption: Another challenge is the acceptance and adoption of AI by employees and customers. Employees may fear that AI will replace their jobs, while customers may be concerned about the privacy of their data and the transparency of automated decisions. Companies should manage these concerns by clearly communicating the benefits of AI, offering training and development programs for employees, and ensuring transparency and data protection for customers.

Initial Investment: Adopting AI often requires a significant initial investment in terms of time, money and resources. Businesses must be prepared to invest in the technology infrastructure, skills and processes needed to integrate AI into their operations. This may include purchasing hardware and software, recruiting AI experts, and implementing training programs for employees. Businesses must also be prepared to deal with the recurring costs of maintaining and updating AI systems.

Security Risks: AI can introduce new security risks, such as adversary attacks and vulnerabilities in machine learning models. Companies must implement robust security measures to protect their AI systems from cyberattacks and malicious manipulation. This may include the use of advanced security techniques, such as data encryption, anomaly detection and continuous systems monitoring.

In conclusion, although AI offers significant benefits to businesses, its adoption also comes with challenges. Businesses must be prepared to invest in the skills, technologies and processes needed to overcome these obstacles and take full advantage of the opportunities offered by AI. By addressing challenges related to data management, talent shortages, technical complexity, ethical and regulatory considerations, and acceptance and adoption, companies can successfully integrate AI into their operations and achieve sustainable competitive advantage.

CHAPTER 3: THE DIFFERENT TYPES OF ARTIFICIAL INTELLIGENCE

3.1 Weak Ai Vs Strong Ai

Weak, or narrow, AI is designed to perform specific tasks, such as facial recognition or language translation. These systems are very efficient in narrow domains, but they lack the general understanding and adaptation capacity of a human mind. For example, a virtual assistant can answer questions about the weather or schedule appointments, but it can't write an essay or invent a new recipe.

Applications of weak AI are many and varied, ranging from personal assistants like Siri and Alexa to recommendation systems on platforms like Netflix and Amazon. In each case, these systems are designed to excel at well-defined tasks, using specialized algorithms that analyze specific data sets to provide precise results. For example, image recognition systems use convolutional neural networks (CNNs) to identify objects in photos, while machine translation systems use recurrent neural networks (RNNs) or transformers to convert text from one language to another.

In contrast, strong, or general, AI aims to possess human cognitive abilities, but it still remains largely theoretical and in development. Strong AI would be able to understand, learn and apply its knowledge flexibly to a variety of tasks. Researchers are working on general AI models, but there are still many challenges to overcome before these systems become a reality. Strong AI should be able to think, reason and make decisions autonomously, not limited to specific areas.

Strong AI research explores advanced concepts such as contextual understanding, abstraction, and knowledge transfer between different tasks. For example, a strong AI system should be able to go from solving a complex math problem to creating a work of art or writing a literary essay. Advances in this area require a deep understanding of human cognition and the mechanisms of learning, as well as significant advances in algorithms and computing infrastructure.

3.2 Supervised Learning

Supervised learning is a method where an algorithm is trained on labeled data. This means that each data input is associated with a correct output, and the algorithm learns to make predictions or classifications based on that data. Common applications of supervised learning include image recognition, spam detection, and demand prediction.

For example, in image recognition, an algorithm can be trained with thousands of labeled images of animals to learn how to distinguish a cat from a dog. Each training image is associated with a label indicating whether the image shows a cat or a dog. The algorithm uses these examples to learn the distinctive characteristics of cats and dogs and can then correctly classify new images.

Supervised learning involves several key steps, including data collection, data preparation, model selection, model training, model evaluation, and model optimization. Data collection involves gathering a large number of labeled examples that represent the problem at hand. Data preparation involves cleaning and transforming data to make it suitable for machine learning. Selecting a model involves choosing an appropriate algorithm for the task, such as a neural network, support vector machine (SVM), or decision tree.

Model training is the process by which the algorithm learns from the labeled data by adjusting its internal parameters to minimize the prediction error. Model evaluation involves testing the trained model on a validation dataset to verify its performance and ability to generalize to new data. Model optimization can include techniques such as hyperparameter tuning, regularization, and the use of ensemble methods to improve model accuracy and robustness.

3.3 Unsupervised Learning

Unsupervised learning involves the analysis of unlabeled data. The algorithm tries to find patterns or relationships in the data without explicit instruction on what to look for. Common techniques include clustering and principal component analysis (PCA).

Clustering is used to group similar data into clusters. For example, a business can use clustering to segment its customers into groups with similar purchasing behaviors. This segmentation can help personalize marketing campaigns and improve customer satisfaction. The most common clustering algorithms include k-means, DBSCAN, and Gaussian mixture models. Each algorithm has its own advantages and disadvantages, and the choice of algorithm depends on the type of data and the objectives of the analysis.

Principal component analysis (PCA) is a technique used to reduce the dimensionality of data while retaining the most important information. This can be useful for visualizing complex data or preparing data for other machine learning algorithms. PCA identifies the principal directions (principal components) in which the data varies the most, and projects the original data onto these new reduced dimensions. This dimensionality reduction makes data easier to interpret and can improve the performance of learning algorithms by reducing noise and redundancy.

Unsupervised learning is particularly useful in situations where it is difficult or expensive to collect labeled data. For example, in anomaly detection applications, normal data is abundant, but examples of anomalies are rare. Unsupervised learning algorithms can analyze normal data to identify typical patterns, and then detect deviations from these patterns as potential anomalies.

3.4 Reinforcement Learning

Reinforcement learning is a technique where an agent learns to make decisions by interacting with an environment. The agent receives rewards or punishments based on its actions and adjusts its strategy to maximize rewards in the long term.

A classic example of reinforcement learning is training an agent to play a video game. The agent starts by taking random actions and receives rewards for successful actions, such as scoring points, and punishments for unsuccessful actions, such as losing a life. Over time, the agent learns to develop strategies to maximize its scores.

Reinforcement learning is based on several key concepts, such as policies, value functions and reward functions. A policy defines how the agent chooses its actions based on the current state of the environment. Value functions estimate the expected value of being in a certain state or taking a certain action in that state, in terms of future rewards. Reward functions define the gains or losses the agent receives after each action.

The most commonly used reinforcement learning algorithms include Q-learning, Policy Gradient learning algorithms, and Actor-Critic methods. Q-learning is an off-policy technique that learns an action value function independent of the policy being followed. Policy learning algorithms, such as policy gradients, directly learn the optimal policy by adjusting parameters to maximize the expected reward. Actor-critic methods combine value and policy approaches using two models: the actor, who chooses actions, and the critic, who evaluates the actions taken by the actor.

Reinforcement learning is used in real-world applications such as recommendation systems, robotics, and autonomous vehicles. For example, self-driving cars use reinforcement learning to navigate roads and avoid obstacles, continually learning from the driving experience. Recommender systems use reinforcement learning to personalize product or content suggestions based on past user interactions, thereby optimizing customer engagement and satisfaction.

In summary, weak AI and strong AI represent two distinct approaches to artificial intelligence, with different practical applications and challenges. Supervised, unsupervised, and reinforcement learning offer complementary methods for training AI systems capable of solving a variety of problems, ranging from image classification to complex decision-making. Advances in these areas continue to transform machine capabilities and expand the horizons of artificial intelligence in business and beyond.

CHAPTER 4: UNDERSTANDING AI ALGORITHMS

4.1 Neural Networks And Deep Learning

Artificial neural networks are inspired by the human brain and are used in deep learning to process complex data. A neural network consists of layers of interconnected neurons, where each neuron receives inputs, processes them, and passes the output to neurons in the next layer. These networks can be simple, with a single hidden layer, or very complex, with dozens or even hundreds of hidden layers, thus forming what are called deep neural networks.

Deep learning uses multi-layer neural networks (deep networks) to learn hierarchical representations of data. This allows deep learning algorithms to process raw data, such as images or text, and extract increasingly abstract features at each layer. For example, in a convolutional neural network (CNN) used for image recognition, early layers can detect edges and textures, while later layers detect more complex patterns like entire objects.

Applications of deep learning include image recognition, speech recognition, machine translation and video games. For example, convolutional neural networks (CNN) are used for image recognition. CNNs are particularly effective for computer vision tasks because they can capture spatial dependencies in images through convolution operations that scan images to detect local patterns. On the other hand, Recurrent Neural Networks (RNN) and Transformers are used for natural language processing. RNNs, which include variants like LSTM (Long Short-Term Memory) and GRU (Gated Recurrent Unit), are capable of handling sequences of data and capturing temporal dependencies, making them ideal for tasks like such as machine translation, text generation and sentiment analysis.

The success of deep learning is largely due to the availability of large amounts of data and the increase in computing power, particularly thanks to GPUs (Graphics Processing Units) and TPUs (Tensor Processing Units). This specialized hardware makes it possible to train deep neural networks on large data sets in reasonable times. Additionally, software frameworks like TensorFlow, PyTorch, and Keras have made the development and deployment of deep learning models more accessible to researchers and practitioners.

4.2 Classification Algorithms

Classification algorithms are used to assign data to predefined categories. Examples include support vector machines (SVM), decision trees, random forests, k-nearest neighbors (k-NN), and neural networks.

Support vector machines (SVM) are classification algorithms that seek to find the best decision boundary (hyperplane) separating different classes in the data. SVMs are effective for binary classification problems and can be adapted for multiclass classification problems using techniques like "one-vs-all" or "one-vs-one". SVMs perform well in high-dimensional spaces and are robust to overfitting problems through the use of regularization.

Decision trees are tree models where each

internal node represents a condition on a feature, each branch represents the result of the condition, and each leaf represents an output class. Decision trees are simple to understand and interpret, and they can handle both categorical and numerical data. However, they are prone to overlearning the training data. Random forests, which are ensembles of decision trees, alleviate this problem by constructing multiple trees from subsamples of the data and averaging their predictions.

k-Nearest Neighbors (k-NN) is a simple but effective classification algorithm where an observation is classified based on the classes of the k closest observations in the feature space. The k-NN is non-parametric and does not require an explicit training phase, but it can be computationally and storage expensive for large datasets.

Neural networks, especially multi-layer neural networks (MLP), are also used for classification tasks. MLPs are capable of learning complex nonlinear representations of data and are particularly effective when combined with advanced regularization and optimization techniques.

4.3 Regression Algorithms

Regression algorithms are used to predict continuous values. Linear regression and logistic regression are among the most commonly used techniques.

Linear regression is used to model the relationship between a continuous dependent variable and one or more independent variables. It seeks to fit a straight line (or a plane in the case of several variables) which minimizes the sum of the squares of the errors. Linear regression is simple to understand and interpret, and it is often used as a starting point for modeling linear relationships between variables.

Logistic regression, although often used for binary classification problems, predicts the probability that an observation belongs to a particular class. It uses a sigmoid function to transform the linear output into probability. Logistic regression is commonly used for applications such as fraud detection, churn prediction, and disease prediction.

Besides these basic techniques, there are many other regression methods, such as polynomial regression, ridge regression, lasso regression (Least Absolute Shrinkage and Selection Operator), and network-based regression methods. of neurons. Polynomial regression allows nonlinear relationships to be modeled by including power terms of the independent variables. Ridge regression and lasso regression add regularization terms to the cost function to penalize the coefficients of the variables and reduce the risk of overfitting.

Neural networks can also be used for regression tasks, especially when the relationships between variables are complex and nonlinear. Deep neural networks can learn hierarchical representations of data and model complex relationships that are difficult to capture with traditional regression models.

4.4 Optimization Algorithms

Optimization algorithms seek to find the best possible solutions within a given set of constraints. Examples include stochastic optimization, genetic algorithms, particle swarm optimization (PSO), and Tabu Search.

Stochastic optimization uses probabilistic methods to find optimal solutions. For example, algorithms like stochastic gradient descent (SGD) optimization are widely used to train machine learning models by minimizing cost functions. SGD updates model parameters iteratively using random samples from the dataset, allowing large datasets to be processed efficiently.

Genetic algorithms are inspired by the theory of evolution and use operations such as selection, crossover and mutation to evolve towards optimal solutions. These algorithms are particularly effective for complex problems with large search spaces, such as optimizing the design of neural networks or planning paths for robots.

Particle swarm optimization (PSO) is a technique inspired by the collective behavior of animals, such as schools of fish or flocks of birds. Particles in the swarm move through the search space adjusting their positions based on their own experience and that of their neighbors, thereby converging toward optimal solutions. PSO is used in applications such as optimizing machine learning model parameters, system design, and combinatorial problem solving.

Tabu Search is an optimization method that uses adaptive memory to avoid already explored solutions and escape local minima. It is often used to solve combinatorial optimization problems, such as the traveling salesman problem (TSP) and production planning.

These optimization algorithms are essential for improving the performance of machine learning models and solving complex problems in various fields. By combining these techniques with machine learning algorithms, companies can develop more robust and efficient AI solutions that can adapt to dynamic environments and changing requirements.

In conclusion, understanding the different types of AI algorithms, such as neural networks and deep learning, classification algorithms, regression algorithms and optimization algorithms, is essential to take full advantage of the potential of artificial intelligence. Each type of algorithm has its own strengths and weaknesses, and the choice of algorithm depends on the problem to be solved, the data available, and the objectives of the analysis. By mastering these algorithms, companies can develop innovative and efficient AI solutions, capable of transforming their operations and creating added value.

PART 2: INTEGRATING AI INTO BUSINESS OPERATIONS

CHAPTER 1: DEVELOPMENT AND IMPLEMENTATION OF AI SOLUTIONS

1.1 Ai Needs Assessment

Before integrating AI into a business, it is essential to assess the specific needs of the business. This involves identifying processes that can benefit from automation or optimization using AI. Companies should also assess their data maturity and determine whether they have the resources to implement AI solutions.

SWOT Analysis : A good starting point is to perform a SWOT (strengths, weaknesses, opportunities and threats) analysis to understand how AI can bring value to the business. For example, an e-commerce company can use AI to improve its product recommendations, while a manufacturing company can use AI to optimize its production lines. A SWOT analysis can reveal areas where AI can improve efficiency, reduce costs and increase customer satisfaction.

Data Maturity Assessment: Data quality and availability are crucial to the success of AI initiatives. Businesses should assess the maturity of their data, including data collection, storage, management and quality. This involves checking whether the data is complete, accurate and accessible. Data management tools and regular audits can help assess and improve data maturity.

Resources and Skills: It is also important to determine whether the company has the necessary resources, both human and technical, to develop and deploy AI solutions. This includes the availability of talent in data science, machine learning engineering and technology project management. Companies should assess their internal skills and, if necessary, consider training employees or recruiting new talent to fill gaps.

1.2 Choice Of Ai Tools And Technologies

Once needs have been assessed, it is important to choose the right tools and technologies to develop and deploy AI solutions. This includes the selection of AI development platforms, machine learning frameworks and cloud infrastructures for hosting AI models.

Machine Learning Frameworks: Popular frameworks include TensorFlow, PyTorch, and scikit-learn, each offering specific features for developing AI models. TensorFlow, developed by Google, is known for its flexibility and ability to handle complex deep learning models. PyTorch, developed by Facebook, is loved for its ease of use and integration with Python, making it a popular choice among researchers. Scikit-learn is a powerful tool for traditional machine learning models and offers a variety of ready-to-use algorithms for classification, regression and clustering.

Cloud Platforms: Cloud platforms like AWS, Google Cloud, and Azure provide machine learning services that make it easier to deploy and manage AI models. AWS offers services such as SageMaker for model development and deployment, as well as data processing and analysis tools. Google Cloud offers services like AI Platform and BigQuery ML, which help develop and train machine learning models at scale. Azure offers Azure Machine Learning, an integrated platform for developing, training, and deploying AI models.

Integration and Compatibility: When choosing tools and technologies, it is important to ensure that they are compatible with the company's existing systems. This includes integration with databases , data management systems and visualization tools. Companies must also consider the scalability and flexibility of the solutions chosen to meet future needs.

1.3 Development Of Ai Models

AI model development begins with data collection and preparation. Data must be cleaned, normalized and formatted for use by machine learning algorithms. Once the data is ready, models can be trained, evaluated and optimized.

Data Collection and Preparation: Data collection involves gathering information from various sources, such as internal databases, IoT sensors, social networks, and third-party APIs. Data preparation includes steps such as cleaning data to eliminate errors and missing values, normalizing data to ensure consistency, and transforming data to fit the needs of machine learning algorithms.

Choice of Algorithms: Model training involves choosing the right algorithms depending on the problem to be solved. This may include classification, regression, clustering or deep learning algorithms. The choice of algorithms depends on the nature of the data, the objectives of the analysis and the performance requirements.

Hyperparameter Adjustment and Model Validation: Once the algorithms have been chosen, the hyperparameters must be adjusted to optimize the performance of the models. Validation techniques, such as cross-validation, are used to evaluate models and ensure that they generalize well to new data. It is crucial to verify that models do not suffer from overfitting, that is, they are not over-fitted to the training data to the detriment of their ability to generalize.

Optimization and Retraining: Models need

to be optimized to improve their accuracy and efficiency. This may include using regularization techniques, tuning hyperparameters, and experimenting with different algorithms. Models also need to be retrained regularly with new data to adapt to changes in the input data and maintain their performance.

1.4 Integration And Deployment

Integrating AI models into existing business systems is a critical step. This may involve developing API interfaces, creating dashboards to visualize model results, and ensuring compatibility with data management systems.

Development of API Interfaces: API interfaces allow AI models to be connected to existing applications and systems. They facilitate the integration of models into business processes and allow end users to access model results transparently. Developing robust, well-documented APIs is essential to ensure smooth integration and effective use of AI models.

Creation of Dashboards: Interactive and

personalized dashboards allow you to visualize the results of AI models and provide actionable insights to decision-makers. Visualization tools, such as Tableau, Power BI, and D3.js, can be used to create intuitive and informative visualizations. Dashboards should be designed to meet specific user needs and facilitate the interpretation of model results.

Model Monitoring and Maintenance: Deploying AI models into production requires continuous monitoring to ensure their performance and accuracy. Companies should have monitoring processes in place to detect model drift, errors, and changes in input data. Models must be retrained regularly with new data to maintain their effectiveness and adapt to changing market conditions.

Ensuring Security and Compliance: Integrating AI models into existing systems must also consider data security and regulatory compliance. Companies must put security measures in place to protect sensitive data and ensure that models comply with applicable laws and regulations, such as GDPR in Europe. This includes implementing access controls, encrypting data and conducting regular security audits.

In conclusion, developing and implementing AI solutions requires careful planning, rigorous assessment of needs and resources, and careful attention to model integration and monitoring. By following these steps, businesses can maximize the benefits of AI, improve their operations, and create added value for their customers and stakeholders.

CHAPTER 2: BUSINESS PROCESS AUTOMATION

2.1 Identification Of Automable Processes

The first step to automating business processes with AI is to identify tasks that can be automated. Repetitive and manual tasks, such as data entry, inventory management, and order processing, are ideal candidates for automation.

To identify these processes, businesses can use process mapping techniques to analyze and document their current workflows. Process mapping involves creating diagrams detailing each step in a process, who is responsible for each step, and the interactions between different stakeholders. This helps identify bottlenecks and inefficiencies that can be resolved through automation.

Task Analysis: Once processes are mapped, companies must analyze each task to determine its automation potential. Tasks that are routine, repetitive and prone to human error are the best candidates. For example, manual data entry into ERP (Enterprise Resource Planning) or CRM (Customer Relationship Management) systems can be automated to reduce errors and free up time for higher value-added activities.

Impact Assessment: It is also crucial to assess the potential impact of automation on operations and employees. This includes a cost and benefit analysis, as well as an assessment of the workforce implications. Businesses must consider not only the efficiency gains, but also the effects on employee and customer satisfaction.

Prioritization of Initiatives: Once processes have been identified and analyzed, companies should prioritize automation initiatives based on their potential impact and feasibility. Processes that offer the most significant gains in efficiency and cost, and are technically feasible, should be prioritized.

2.2 Automation Of Repetitive Tasks

Automating repetitive tasks frees up time for employees, who can focus on higher value-added activities. Chatbots, for example, can automate first-level customer support, answering frequently asked questions and handling common requests. Chatbots use natural language processing (NLP) to understand and respond to customer queries, thereby improving customer service efficiency and user satisfaction.

Robotic Process Automation (RPA): Software robots, or RPA (Robotic Process Automation), can be used to automate administrative tasks such as invoicing, payment management and updating databases. RPAs mimic human actions and can interact with IT systems in the same way an employee would. For example, an RPA bot can pull billing data from different systems, consolidate it, and generate financial reports, reducing the time needed for these tasks and minimizing errors.

Workflow Automation: Workflow automation involves the use of software to orchestrate tasks and processes within the business. This includes business process management (BPM), where automated systems can track and manage end-to-end processes. For example, a BPM system can automate the online ordering process, from order receipt to delivery, including inventory management and invoicing.

Example Applications: In the healthcare industry, RPA can be used to automate data entry of electronic medical records, allowing doctors and nurses to devote more time to patient care. In banking, RPAs can automate compliance verification and loan application processing, speeding up the process and reducing operational costs.

2.3 Optimization Of Production And Logistics

AI can optimize production lines by predicting machine failures, planning maintenance operations and adjusting production parameters in real time. Machine learning algorithms can analyze sensor data to detect anomalies and prevent failures before they occur.

Predictive Maintenance: Predictive maintenance uses AI to monitor machine health and predict potential failures before they occur. IoT sensors installed on equipment collect real-time data on vibration, temperature and other parameters. Machine learning algorithms analyze this data to identify failure patterns and recommend proactive maintenance interventions. This helps reduce unplanned downtime and maximize equipment lifespan.

Production Optimization: AI can adjust production parameters in real time to maximize efficiency and quality. For example, in the manufacturing industry, optimization algorithms can adjust machine speeds, processing temperatures, and material flows to improve yields and reduce waste. Advanced process control (APC) systems use predictive models to anticipate and correct process variations, ensuring consistent, high-quality production.

Logistics and Inventory Management: In logistics, AI can be used to optimize delivery routes, reduce transportation costs and improve inventory management. Warehouse management systems (WMS) using AI can forecast demand, plan replenishments, and organize storage spaces more efficiently. Supply chain optimization algorithms can analyze sales and inventory data to predict future needs, minimizing inventory costs and out-of-stock risks.

Example Applications: In the retail sector, AI can optimize delivery routes by taking into account real-time traffic conditions, delivery constraints and customer preferences. For example, UPS uses optimization algorithms to plan the routes of its delivery trucks, reducing distances traveled and carbon emissions. In manufacturing, companies like Siemens are using AI to optimize production processes and reduce operational costs.

2.4 Impact Of Automation On Employment

Business process automation can have a significant impact on employment. If certain tasks become obsolete, new roles emerge to manage and oversee automated systems. Employees must be trained to learn new skills and adapt to technological changes.

Role Transformation: Automation transforms the nature of work by eliminating routine and repetitive tasks, but it also creates new opportunities for higher value-added roles. For example, data analysts, AI engineers and cybersecurity experts are increasingly in demand to manage and supervise automated systems. Employees can be redeployed to tasks that are creative, strategic and require interpersonal skills, such as product innovation, project management and customer relationship development.

Training and Development: Companies must take a proactive approach to change management, clearly communicating the benefits of automation and offering training and professional development programs. This can help alleviate employee concerns and ease the transition to an automated work environment. Training programs may include courses on AI technologies, data science skills, and change management best practices.

Organizational Adaptation: Companies must also adapt their organizational structures to reap the benefits of automation. This may include the creation of new departments or teams dedicated to technological innovation, data management and cybersecurity. Companies must encourage a culture of innovation and continuous learning to ensure their employees are ready to adapt to technological developments.

Example Applications: In healthcare, electronic health record automation frees up time for doctors and nurses, allowing them to focus on patient care. In the banking industry, automating compliance processes reduces employee workload and improves operational efficiency.

In conclusion, business process automation with AI offers significant opportunities to improve efficiency, reduce costs and create added value for customers and stakeholders. However, it requires careful planning, proactive change management and investment in employee training and skills development. By taking a strategic approach to automation, businesses can maximize the benefits of AI and prepare their workforce for the future of work.

CHAPTER 3: DATA MANAGEMENT AND AI

3.1 Data Collection And Preparation

Data collection and preparation are essential steps in developing AI solutions. Data must be collected from a variety of sources, including internal databases, IoT sensors, social networks, and third-party APIs. This diversity of sources helps capture a complete and accurate view of customer operations and behaviors.

Data Sources: Internal databases contain critical information about company operations, sales, inventory and customers. IoT (Internet of Things) sensors provide real-time data about equipment, machines, and physical environments. Social media offers valuable insights into customer preferences and opinions. Third-party APIs provide access to external data such as demographic, economic and weather information.

Data Cleaning: Once the data is collected, it

needs to be cleaned to remove errors, duplicates and missing values. Data cleaning is a crucial step because faulty data can lead to inaccurate AI models and incorrect business decisions. Cleanup techniques include removing incorrect entries, correcting typographical errors, and handling missing values by imputing or removing them.

Normalization and Scaling: Normalization and scaling of data are also important to ensure that the data is consistent and ready for use by machine learning algorithms. Normalization involves transforming data so that it has a similar distribution, often by scaling it to a standard range such as 0 to 1. This helps algorithms converge faster and improve their performance. Data scaling involves adjusting feature values to ensure that no single feature dominates the others due to its different scale.

Advanced Exploration and Preparation: Once data is cleaned and normalized, it can be explored to identify patterns, trends, and relationships. Data mining techniques include descriptive analysis, graphical visualizations, and inferential statistics. This exploration helps in understanding the data and preparing specific datasets for training AI models.

3.2 Data Quality And Bias Management

Data quality is crucial for the success of AI models. Poor data quality can lead to biased or inaccurate models, which can negatively impact business decisions. Companies must implement rigorous data quality management processes.

Audits and Data Validation: Companies should conduct regular audits to verify the accuracy, completeness and relevance of data. Validation mechanisms include consistency testing, cross-checking with independent data sources, and statistical analysis to detect anomalies and errors.

Bias Management: Bias management is essential to ensure that AI models make fair and non-discriminatory decisions. Bias can arise at different stages, including data collection, data preparation and modeling. Techniques for managing bias include balancing datasets, using fair metrics for model evaluation, and auditing models to detect biased behavior.

Monitoring and Continuous Improvement: Data quality should be continuously monitored, and businesses should implement continuous improvement processes to respond to data quality issues as they arise. This includes updating data collection procedures, training staff on the importance of data quality, and investing in advanced data management technologies.

3.3 Data Storage And Security

Data storage must be secure to protect user privacy and comply with data protection regulations. Businesses can use cloud storage solutions, which offer scalability and cost benefits while ensuring security and compliance.

Storage Solutions: Cloud storage solutions, such as AWS S3, Google Cloud Storage, and Azure Blob Storage, allow large amounts of data to be stored securely and scalably. These solutions provide redundancy, backup and disaster recovery capabilities, ensuring continuous data availability.

Data Security Practices: Data security practices include encryption of data in transit and at rest to protect sensitive information from unauthorized access. Multi-factor authentication (MFA) is used to strengthen the security of access to data systems. Continuous monitoring of access and suspicious activity helps detect and prevent security breaches.

Data Governance Policies: Having data governance policies in place helps define responsibilities and processes to manage and protect data effectively. Policies should include guidelines on data collection, storage, use and deletion, as well as procedures for responding to security incidents and user requests regarding their personal data.

3.4 Analysis And Interpretation Of Data

Data analysis helps uncover valuable insights and make informed decisions. Data analysis techniques include data visualization, descriptive statistics, and machine learning methods.

Data Visualization: Data visualization tools, such as Tableau, Power BI and D3.js, help businesses interpret data and communicate results to stakeholders. Interactive visualizations allow you to explore data from different angles and uncover hidden insights. Graphs, charts, and dashboards help present results clearly and concisely.

Descriptive Statistics: Descriptive statistics summarize the main characteristics of the data, such as means, medians, standard deviations and distributions. These analyzes help to understand the structure of the data and identify general trends. For example, businesses can use descriptive statistics to analyze customer behaviors, sales performance, and market trends.

Machine Learning Methods: Machine learning algorithms can be used to identify trends, predict future outcomes, and optimize business processes. Supervised learning techniques, such as linear regression and decision trees, are used to predict values and classify data. Unsupervised learning techniques, such as clustering and principal component analysis (PCA), are used to discover hidden patterns and structures in data.

Communication of Results : It is essential to communicate the results of analyzes in a clear and understandable manner to stakeholders. Reports, presentations and interactive dashboards are effective tools for sharing insights and recommendations. Good communication helps align business decisions with data-driven insights and ensure actions are taken based on analysis results.

In conclusion, data management is a crucial aspect of the development and integration of AI solutions. Rigorous data collection and preparation, quality and bias management, secure storage, and in-depth analysis are essential to ensure the success of AI initiatives. By adopting robust data management practices, businesses can maximize the value of their data and make more informed and strategic decisions.

CHAPTER 4: SECURITY AND AI

4.1 Security Threats Related To Ai

The use of AI introduces new security threats that require increased vigilance and sophisticated defense strategies. AI models can be targeted by adversarial attacks, where malicious data is introduced to trick the model and cause incorrect results. For example, a slight alteration of an image can lead an image recognition model to misidentify an object. These attacks can compromise the reliability of AI systems and have serious consequences, particularly in critical applications such as facial recognition or autonomous driving.

Adversarial Attacks: Cybercriminals can exploit vulnerabilities in AI systems to access sensitive data or disrupt operations. Adversarial attacks can include the generation of adversarial examples specifically designed to fool AI models. For example, by adding imperceptible noise to an image, an attacker can cause an image recognition model to incorrectly identify the image.

Model Stealing: AI models themselves can be targets for theft. Attackers can attempt to steal proprietary AI models using techniques such as model inversion or model extraction. Model inversion involves using model outputs to reconstruct the original inputs, while model extraction involves creating a similar model by querying the target model.

Data Exploitation: Cybercriminals can also exploit the data used to train AI models. Sensitive or personal data can be compromised if appropriate security measures are not put in place. For example, attackers can intercept data in transit or access poorly secured databases.

Security Measures: Companies must be aware of these threats and implement robust security measures to protect their AI systems. This includes continuously monitoring AI systems to detect anomalies, using adversarial defense techniques to make models more robust against attacks, and implementing strict security policies to control access to models. and data.

4.2 Security Strategies For Ai Systems

Security strategies for AI systems include several technical and organizational measures aimed at protecting AI models and the data they use.

Rigorous Validation of Input Data: Validation of input data is essential to prevent adversarial attacks and guarantee the integrity of AI models. Businesses should implement filters and controls to verify that input data is correct and does not contain malicious content. This may include anomaly detection techniques to identify and block suspicious entries.

Isolation of Environments: Isolating training and deployment environments for AI models can help minimize security risks. Isolated environments prevent attackers from accessing models and sensitive data. For example, models can be trained in secure cloud environments, with strict access controls and regular audits.

Encryption of Models and Data: Encryption is a key measure to protect AI models and the data they use. Data must be encrypted in transit and at rest to prevent unauthorized access. AI models can also be encrypted to protect their intellectual property and prevent model theft.

Identity and Access Management (IAM): Having identity and access management policies in place is crucial to controlling who can access AI systems and what actions they can perform. Businesses should use IAM solutions to manage user identities, control access to resources, and monitor suspicious activity. Multi-factor authentication (MFA) can enhance access security.

DevOps Security (DevSecOps): Security should be integrated into the AI model development lifecycle, a practice known as DevSecOps. This includes using automated security testing during development, validating models before deployment, and continuously monitoring systems in production. DevSecOps teams collaborate to ensure AI models are secure from design and throughout their lifecycle.

4.3 Compliance And Regulations

Businesses must comply with data protection laws and regulations, such as GDPR in Europe and CCPA in California. These regulations require companies to protect users' personal data and respect their privacy rights.

GDPR (General Data Protection Regulation): The GDPR imposes strict obligations on companies that collect, process and store personal data of EU residents. Companies must obtain explicit consent from users to collect their data, provide clear information on the use of the data and allow users to exercise their rights (e.g. access, rectification and deletion of data). GDPR violations can result in significant fines.

CCPA (California Consumer Privacy Act): The CCPA gives California residents similar data protection rights, including the right to know what personal information is collected, the right to request deletion of their data, and the right to opt-out the sale of their personal information. Businesses must comply with CCPA requirements and have processes in place to respond to consumer requests.

Data Governance Policies: Having data governance policies in place helps ensure compliance with data protection regulations. These policies should define employee responsibilities, data management processes and security measures to protect personal data. Training employees on security and compliance practices is also essential to minimize the risk of data breaches.

Audits and Assessments: Companies should conduct regular audits to assess their compliance with regulations and identify gaps in their data protection practices. Data Protection Impact Assessments (DPIAs) can help identify risks associated with the processing of personal data and put measures in place to mitigate them.

4.4 Data Security And Confidentiality

Data security and privacy are major concerns for businesses using AI. Businesses must put data protection measures in place to ensure the security and confidentiality of personal and sensitive information.

Data Encryption: Encryption of data in transit and at rest is essential to protect sensitive information from unauthorized access. Encryption in transit protects data as it is transferred between systems, while encryption at rest protects stored data. Businesses must use strong encryption protocols and manage encryption keys securely.

Data Anonymization: Anonymizing sensitive data can help protect user privacy. Anonymization involves removing or changing personal information to prevent individuals from being identified. Anonymization techniques include removing direct identifiers, generalizing data, and adding noise to the data.

Access Controls: Implementing strict access controls is essential to protect sensitive data. Companies should define access policies based on employee roles and responsibilities, and use IAM solutions to manage access to systems and data. Multi-factor authentication (MFA) and continuous monitoring of user activities can help detect and prevent unauthorized access.

Security Incident Management: Security incident management and data breach preparedness are crucial to minimizing the impacts of security incidents. Companies must have incident response plans in place to quickly detect, contain and remediate data breaches. These plans must include procedures for informing data protection authorities and relevant stakeholders, as well as measures to mitigate the consequences of breaches.

Awareness and Training: Raising awareness and training employees on data security and privacy is essential to creating a culture of security within the company. Training programs should cover security best practices, regulatory obligations and procedures to follow in the event of a security incident. Regular training and awareness campaigns can help reinforce secure behaviors and reduce the risk of data breaches.

In conclusion, security of AI systems and data is a crucial aspect of integrating AI into business operations. Companies must implement robust strategies to protect their AI systems from security threats, comply with data protection regulations, and ensure the confidentiality of sensitive information. By adopting rigorous security and governance practices, businesses can minimize risks and maximize the benefits of AI.

Part 3: Practical Applications of AI for Business

CHAPTER 1: IMPROVING CUSTOMER SERVICE WITH AI

1.1 Chatbots And Virtual Assistants

Chatbots and virtual assistants use natural language processing (NLP) to understand and answer customer questions in real time. These tools can automate first-line customer support, reduce wait times, and provide consistent and timely responses to common inquiries.

Features of Chatbots: Chatbots are programmed to handle a variety of common queries, such as tracking orders, resolving billing issues, and providing product information. For example, a customer can interact with a chatbot on a company's website to check the status of their order without needing to speak to a human agent. Chatbots can also be integrated with popular messaging platforms like Facebook Messenger, WhatsApp, and Slack, allowing customers to ask questions and get answers instantly.

Advanced Virtual Assistants: Virtual assistants, like Siri, Alexa and Google Assistant, go beyond simple text interactions by offering voice capabilities and performing more complex tasks. For example, Alexa can schedule appointments, send messages, control smart home devices, and even place online orders. These assistants use advanced NLP algorithms to understand voice commands and interact with users in a more natural and intuitive way.

Benefits for Businesses: Using chatbots and virtual assistants allows businesses to provide 24/7 customer service, reducing wait times and improving customer satisfaction. By automating repetitive tasks, these tools free up time for human agents, who can focus on more complex problems requiring human intervention.

1.2 Personalization Of The Customer Experience

AI helps personalize the customer experience by analyzing customer data to understand their preferences and behaviors. Recommendation systems, for example, use machine learning algorithms to suggest products or services based on past purchases and interactions with the company.

Recommendation Systems: Recommendation systems are commonly used by streaming platforms, e-commerce sites and social media services. For example, Netflix uses machine learning algorithms to recommend movies and series based on users' viewing habits. Amazon suggests products based on previous purchases and viewed items, increasing the likelihood of purchase.

Personalization of Marketing Communications: Businesses can also use AI to personalize marketing communications, sending targeted offers and relevant content to each customer. For example, a business can analyze customer purchasing and browsing data to send personalized emails with special offers or product recommendations. This improves customer satisfaction and increases conversion rates because messages are tailored to each customer's specific interests and needs.

Segmentation and Predictive Analysis: AI also makes it possible to segment customers into homogeneous groups based on their behaviors and preferences. Predictive analytics algorithms can anticipate future customer needs and identify cross-selling and up-selling opportunities. For example, a retail company can use AI to predict which products will be popular during the holiday season and plan targeted marketing campaigns accordingly.

1.3 Complaints Management And Technical Support

AI can automate complaints management and technical support by using natural language processing algorithms to analyze customer inquiries and direct them to the appropriate resources.

Automatic Categorization and Assignment: An AI system can categorize support tickets based on the nature of the problem (e.g. technical problem, billing question, refund request) and assign them to the appropriate agents. This ensures that each request is handled by the most qualified person, improving efficiency and customer satisfaction.

Automated Solutions: AI-based help desk tools can also provide automated solutions to common problems. For example, a virtual assistant can guide a customer through troubleshooting steps to resolve a technical issue without needing the intervention of a human agent. This reduces agent workload and improves the speed of problem resolution.

Complaints Tracking and Analysis: AI also helps track and analyze complaints to identify trends and recurring issues. Businesses can use these insights to improve their products and services, and to train support agents on common issues. For example, if a significant number of complaints relate to the same product, the company can investigate to identify and resolve the underlying cause.

1.4 Case Studies: Customer Service And Ai

Many companies have successfully improved their customer service using AI.

H&M: H&M uses a chatbot to help customers find clothes and track their orders. The chatbot uses NLP to understand customer questions and provide relevant answers. For example, a customer can ask the chatbot to find a red dress in size M, and the chatbot can search the inventory and provide real-time recommendations. This improves customer satisfaction by providing quick and accurate responses.

Alibaba: E-commerce company Alibaba uses AI to personalize product recommendations and optimize marketing campaigns. Through the analysis of customer data, Alibaba can provide personalized offers and product suggestions, thereby increasing sales and customer loyalty. For example, Alibaba analyzes user purchasing behaviors and preferences to send personalized notifications about special offers and new collections.

Sephora: Sephora has integrated a virtual assistant into its website and mobile app to help customers find beauty products and receive personalized recommendations. The assistant uses NLP to understand customer needs and suggest products tailored to their skin type, makeup preferences, and specific concerns. This personalization improves the shopping experience and helps customers make more informed decisions.

Ryanair: The airline Ryanair uses AI to improve customer support and optimize reservation operations. A chatbot helps customers book flights, manage their reservations and get information about company policies. AI also analyzes customer data to send personalized offers and flight updates in real time.

In conclusion, integrating AI into customer service offers significant opportunities to improve efficiency, personalize interactions, and increase customer satisfaction. By using chatbots, virtual assistants, recommendation systems, and automated help desk tools, businesses can provide high-quality customer service while optimizing their resources.

CHAPTER 2: MARKETING AND SALES OPTIMIZATION

2.1 Predictive Analysis And Market Segmentation

AI helps optimize marketing campaigns by using predictive analytics to anticipate consumer behaviors and segment the market more precisely. Machine learning algorithms can analyze historical data to identify trends and patterns, helping businesses target the most promising market segments.

Using Historical Data: Businesses can leverage years of historical data to understand past consumer behaviors. For example, a retail business can analyze customer purchasing trends to predict which products will be popular in upcoming seasons and adjust its inventory accordingly. Analyzing purchase histories, website visits and social media interactions can reveal behavioral patterns that help predict future demand.

Market Segmentation: AI-based market segmentation also helps personalize marketing messages for different customer groups. For example, a business can segment its customers based on their purchasing habits, product preferences, and online behaviors. Using clustering algorithms, like k-means, businesses can identify customer segments with similar characteristics and tailor their marketing strategies for each segment, increasing campaign effectiveness.

Personalized Campaigns: Once market segments are identified, businesses can create personalized marketing campaigns for each group. For example, a segment of young professionals may receive deals on technology products, while a segment of parents may receive promotions on children's items. This personalization increases the relevance of messages and improves conversion rates.

2.2 Targeted Advertising And Product Recommendations

AI algorithms are used to target ads more

effectively by analyzing users' online behaviors and identifying the best opportunities to serve ads.

Targeted Advertising: AI-based advertising systems analyze users' browsing data, social media interactions, and purchase histories to deliver relevant ads at the right time. For example, Google Ads uses machine learning algorithms to target users with ads based on their recent searches and online behaviors. This increases the likelihood that users will click on the ads and make a purchase.

Product Recommendations: Recommender systems use collaborative filtering and content-based filtering techniques to suggest relevant products or services to users. For example, Amazon recommends products based on customers' past purchases and items viewed. Streaming platforms like Netflix and Spotify use AI to recommend movies, series or songs based on users' preferences and viewing or listening histories. These personalized recommendations increase user engagement and customer satisfaction.

Improved Engagement: AI-powered personalized recommendations can also increase time spent on platforms and improve user experience. For example, Netflix uses algorithms to analyze viewing behavior and recommend content that each user might like, increasing the likelihood that they will continue using the service.

2.3 Optimization Of Marketing Campaigns

AI can optimize marketing campaigns by analyzing real-time data to adjust strategies and maximize results.

Marketing Automation: AI-powered marketing automation platforms can manage email blasts, social media ads, and content campaigns, tailoring messages and offers based on customer feedback. For example, a marketing automation platform can analyze email open and click rates to adjust content and sending times, thereby optimizing engagement and conversions.

A/B Testing and Experimentation: AI tools

can also perform A/B testing to determine which campaign variations are most effective. By testing different versions of messages, visuals and CTAs (Call-to-Action), businesses can identify which elements generate the most conversions. The insights obtained from these tests make it possible to optimize campaigns and improve marketing performance.

Real-Time Analytics: Real-time analytics allows businesses to monitor campaign performance and make instant adjustments. For example, a social media advertising campaign can be adjusted in real time based on click-through rates and conversions, allowing budget to be allocated to the best performing ads.

2.4 Performance Monitoring And Analysis

Monitoring and analyzing the performance of marketing campaigns is essential to evaluate their effectiveness and make adjustments.

Interactive Dashboards: AI-powered analytics tools can create interactive dashboards that allow marketers to view campaign results in real-time. These dashboards can display key performance indicators (KPIs) such as conversion rate, return on investment (ROI), and user engagement. For example, Google Analytics offers custom dashboards to track online campaign performance.

Sentiment Analysis and Feedback: AI can also analyze consumer sentiments from social media and online reviews to assess the impact of marketing campaigns. For example, natural language processing (NLP) algorithms can analyze user comments to identify positive and negative sentiments, providing insights into audience perception of campaigns.

Recommendations for Optimization: AI algorithms can provide recommendations for optimizing future campaigns by identifying best practices and opportunities for improvement. For example, an analysis of previous campaign performance may reveal that certain images or messages are more effective for certain market segments, allowing future marketing strategies to be adjusted.

In conclusion, integrating AI into marketing operations helps optimize campaigns, personalize customer interactions and improve business performance. By using predictive analytics, targeted advertising, campaign optimization and performance monitoring, businesses can maximize their ROI and deliver an exceptional customer experience.

CHAPTER 3: AI IN HUMAN RESOURCES MANAGEMENT

3.1 Recruitment And Selection Of Talent

AI can transform the recruitment process by automating candidate pre-screening, analyzing CVs and identifying key skills. Machine learning algorithms can evaluate applications based on defined criteria and recommend the best candidates for interviews.

Automated Pre-Screening: AI-powered recruitment systems can quickly filter thousands of applications, identifying relevant qualifications, experience and skills. For example, algorithms can analyze resumes and cover letters to extract key information, such as technical skills, years of experience, and professional achievements. This automation allows recruiters to focus on the qualitative assessment of shortlisted candidates.

Recruitment Chatbots: Recruitment chatbots can interact with candidates, answer their questions and guide them through the application process. For example, a chatbot can ask screening questions, provide information about the company and available positions, and schedule interviews. This improves the candidate experience by providing immediate assistance and reducing the time it takes to fill open positions.

Skills and Match Analysis: Machine learning algorithms can compare candidate skills to open position requirements and assess their suitability. AI systems can also analyze LinkedIn profiles and online portfolios to get a more comprehensive view of candidate skills and experiences. For example, an AI system can identify candidates with rare or in-demand skills and rank them based on how well they match the job criteria.

Reducing Bias: AI can also help reduce bias in recruitment by standardizing the pre-screening process. Algorithms can be designed to evaluate applications based on objective criteria, minimizing the influence of unconscious bias. However, it is essential to regularly monitor and adjust models to ensure that they do not reproduce existing biases in the training data.

3.2 Employee Training And Development

AI can personalize employee training and development programs based on their needs and performance. AI-powered training platforms can recommend relevant courses and training modules, track employee progress, and tailor content based on their skills and goals.

Personalized Training Programs: Online learning platforms using AI can analyze employee performance and development needs to recommend personalized training paths. For example, if an employee has specific technical skills gaps, AI can suggest relevant online courses, tutorials, and workshops to fill those gaps. AI systems can also adjust training content based on employees' progress, offering more advanced modules as they learn new skills.

Progress Tracking and Feedback: AI can track employee progress in real time, analyzing their course attendance, assessment scores, and overall engagement. Managers can receive detailed reports on employee performance, identifying areas where improvement is needed and providing constructive feedback. For example, a training platform can send notifications to employees and their supervisors about modules completed, scores earned, and recommended next steps.

Simulations and Virtual Reality (VR) Environments: AI-powered simulations and virtual reality (VR) environments can provide immersive training experiences, allowing employees to practice real-world scenarios in a safe, controlled environment. For example, a VR simulation can be used to train employees on safety procedures, complex technical skills, or difficult customer interactions. These simulations provide hands-on, interactive learning, improving knowledge retention and employee confidence.

3.3 Performance Management And Retention

AI can help evaluate employee performance by analyzing productivity data, feedback, and reviews. AI-powered performance management systems can provide insights into each employee's strengths and areas for improvement, facilitating constructive discussions and professional development.

Performance Assessment: AI systems can analyze various data sources, such as productivity reports, performance reviews, peer feedback, and satisfaction surveys. For example, a machine learning algorithm can identify trends and patterns in performance data to evaluate employee contributions and provide recommendations for improving their performance. Managers can use these insights to conduct more objective, data-driven performance reviews.

Turnover Prevention: Machine learning algorithms can also predict employee departure risks by analyzing trends and behaviors. For example, an AI system can identify warning signs of disengagement, such as decreased productivity, frequent absences, or negative feedback. Companies can use this information to implement retention strategies, such as recognition and reward programs, career development opportunities and wellness initiatives.

Personalized Development Plans: AI systems can help create personalized development plans for each employee, identifying skills to develop and relevant training opportunities. For example, an employee who shows leadership potential may receive recommendations for management courses, mentorships and development projects. These personalized development plans help employees advance in their careers and achieve their professional goals.

3.4 Forecasting Labor Needs

AI can help businesses predict their workforce needs by analyzing market trends, business cycles and internal data. Predictive models can estimate future labor demand, identify needed skills, and plan recruitment accordingly.

Market Trend Analysis: AI algorithms can analyze economic data, industry trends, and growth forecasts to estimate future labor demand. For example, a technology company can use AI to predict an increase in demand for software developers due to technological advancements and future projects. These forecasts allow companies to plan their recruitment and training programs accordingly.

Resource Planning: Businesses can also use AI to optimize work schedule planning, taking into account fluctuations in demand and employee availability. For example, an AI-powered scheduling system can adjust employee schedules based on peak demand, planned time off, and individual preferences. This helps ensure that human resources are allocated efficiently and operations run smoothly.

Labor Cost Optimization: Predictive models can help identify opportunities to reduce labor costs by optimizing resource allocation and minimizing overtime. For example, a retail company can use AI to predict periods of low activity and adjust schedules accordingly, reducing labor costs without compromising service quality.

In conclusion, the integration of AI into human resources management can transform recruitment, training, performance management and resource planning processes.

By using machine learning algorithms and AI systems, companies can improve efficiency, reduce bias, personalize development programs, and optimize human resource allocation. These innovations help companies attract, develop and retain top talent, while adapting to changing market needs.

CHAPTER 4: FINANCIAL MANAGEMENT AND AI

4.1 Financial Forecasting And Analysis

AI can improve financial forecasting and analysis by using machine learning algorithms to analyze historical data and predict future performance. Predictive models can estimate revenue, costs and cash flow, helping businesses plan budgets and make informed financial decisions.

Predictive Models: Machine learning algorithms, such as recurrent neural networks (RNN) and time series models, can analyze historical financial data to predict future performance. For example, a predictive model can estimate quarterly revenue by analyzing past sales trends, business cycles, and seasonal factors. Businesses can use these forecasts to plan budgets, allocate resources and set realistic financial goals.

Identifying Trends and Anomalies: AI-based

financial analysis tools can identify trends and anomalies in financial data. For example, anomaly detection algorithms can spot unusual variations in operational costs or cash flows, alerting financial managers to potential problems or optimization opportunities. These insights allow businesses to respond quickly and take corrective action before problems become worse.

Recommendations to Improve Profitability: AI systems can provide recommendations on actions to take to improve profitability. For example, a detailed cost and revenue analysis can reveal areas where expenses can be reduced or where sales efforts can be intensified to maximize revenue. Businesses can use these recommendations to adjust their strategies and improve their overall financial performance.

4.2 Fraud Detection

AI is particularly effective at detecting fraud by analyzing transactions in real time and identifying suspicious behavior. Machine learning algorithms can learn from known fraud patterns and detect anomalous activity that could indicate fraud.

Real-Time Analysis: AI-based fraud detection systems can analyze thousands of transactions in real time, using anomaly detection algorithms to identify suspicious transactions. For example, an AI system can detect an unusual credit card transaction, such as a large purchase in a foreign country shortly after a small local transaction, and immediately alert the appropriate authorities.

Supervised and Unsupervised Learning Models: Supervised learning algorithms can be trained on datasets containing fraud examples to learn to recognize specific fraud patterns. Unsupervised learning algorithms, such as clustering, can identify atypical transactions without the need for previously labeled examples. These complementary techniques make it possible to cover a wide range of potential fraud scenarios.

Anomaly Detection Techniques: AI-based fraud detection systems use anomaly detection techniques to identify unusual transactions. For example, clustering and regression models can identify deviations from normal behavior, flagging potentially fraudulent activity. This allows businesses to respond quickly to prevent financial losses and protect sensitive information.

4.3 Optimization Of Investments

AI can help optimize investment portfolios by analyzing market data, assessing risks, and recommending investment strategies. Robo-advisors use machine learning algorithms to create personalized portfolios based on investors' financial goals and risk tolerance.

Market Data Analysis: Machine learning algorithms can analyze vast amounts of market data, including stock prices, economic indicators and financial news, to identify investment opportunities. For example, an AI model can analyze historical stock data to predict their future performance and recommend the most promising stocks to include in an investment portfolio.

Risk Assessment: AI algorithms can assess the risks associated with different investments by taking into account factors such as market volatility, correlations between assets and economic trends. For example, a robo-advisor can use Monte Carlo simulation models to evaluate risk scenarios and recommend diversification strategies to minimize risks while maximizing potential returns.

Personalized Recommendations : AI-powered robo-advisors can create personalized portfolios based on investors' financial goals and risk tolerance. For example, a conservative investor may receive recommendations for a diversified portfolio with low volatility, while an aggressive investor may be offered a portfolio with high-yielding stocks and growth opportunities. Personalized recommendations help investors achieve their financial goals while respecting their risk profile.

Continuous Optimization: AI enables continuous optimization of portfolios by monitoring asset performance in real time and adjusting allocations based on market conditions. For example, an AI system can recommend rebalancing a portfolio by selling overvalued assets and buying undervalued assets, in order to maintain an optimal allocation based on the investor's financial goals.

4.4 Financial Risk Management

Financial risk management is crucial for business stability and growth. AI can analyze economic data, market trends and performance indicators to assess risks and recommend risk management strategies.

Economic and Market Data Analysis: AI algorithms can analyze complex economic data, such as interest rates, commodity prices and macroeconomic indicators, to assess financial risks. For example, an AI model can predict the impact of interest rate fluctuations on a company's borrowing costs and recommend hedging strategies to mitigate risks.

Predictive Risk Models: AI-based risk models can predict fluctuations in asset prices, changes in exchange rates and the impacts of global economic events. For example, a risk model can use neural networks to predict commodity price movements based on historical data and market trends. These predictions help businesses make informed decisions to mitigate risks and protect their financial assets.

Risk Management Strategies: AI can recommend risk management strategies based on data analysis and predictive models. For example, a company exposed to currency risks can use AI-based recommendations to implement currency hedges, such as futures or options, to protect profit margins. Companies can also use AI to evaluate the effectiveness of their risk management strategies and adjust their approaches based on the results.

Real-Time Monitoring and Adaptation: AI systems enable real-time monitoring of financial risks, by continuously analyzing market data and performance indicators. For example, a risk management system can monitor a company's trading positions and trigger alerts if defined risk thresholds are exceeded. This proactive monitoring allows companies to respond quickly to market changes and adjust their risk management strategies accordingly.

In conclusion, integrating AI into financial management allows businesses to improve forecasting, detect fraud, optimize investments, and manage risks more effectively. By using machine learning algorithms and AI systems, businesses can make more informed financial decisions, protect their assets and improve their overall performance.

PART 4: STRATEGIES AND FUTURE OF AI IN BUSINESS

CHAPTER 1: DEVELOPING AN AI STRATEGY FOR YOUR BUSINESS

1.1 Development Of An Ai Roadmap

Developing an effective AI strategy starts with developing a detailed roadmap that defines the goals, steps, and resources needed to integrate AI into business operations. The roadmap should include a needs assessment, opportunity and risk analysis, and an action plan for implementation.

Needs Assessment: The first step is to assess the business's AI needs. This involves identifying areas where AI can provide the most value, such as automating processes, improving decision-making, or optimizing the customer experience. Companies should also assess their data maturity, as high-quality data is essential for the success of AI initiatives.

Analysis of Opportunities and Risks: It is important to carry out a thorough analysis of the opportunities and risks related to the adoption of AI. Opportunities may include efficiency gains, cost savings and competitive advantages. Risks may include concerns about security, data privacy and employment impact. A SWOT (strengths, weaknesses, opportunities and threats) analysis can be useful for this step.

Action Plan: Once the needs and opportunities/risks have been assessed, companies must develop a detailed action plan for AI implementation. This includes defining priority projects, allocating necessary resources, and establishing a timeline for each stage. The action plan should also include strategies for change management and employee training.

Key Performance Indicators (KPIs): Companies should define KPIs to measure the success of their AI initiatives. KPIs can include operational performance measures, customer satisfaction indicators, and financial measures. It is important to monitor these KPIs regularly and use them to adjust the AI strategy based on the results obtained.

1.2 Identification Of Strategic Objectives

AI strategic goals should be aligned with business vision and priorities. This can include improving operational efficiency, optimizing customer experience, innovating products and services, and improving decision-making.

Setting Goals: Companies should set clear, measurable goals for each AI initiative. For example, a goal might be to reduce order processing time by 20% through automation, or increase online sales by 15% using AI-based recommendation systems. Goals should be specific, measurable, achievable, relevant and time-bound (SMART).

Organizational Alignment: It is crucial to ensure that all levels of the organization understand and support the goals of AI. This may require communications and training efforts to make employees aware of the benefits of AI and involve them in the implementation process. Leaders must lead by example by actively supporting AI initiatives and encouraging a culture of innovation.

Strategic Priorities: Strategic objectives must

be aligned with the overall priorities of the company. For example, if one of the company's priorities is to improve the customer experience, AI initiatives should focus on areas such as automated customer service, personalization of offers, and improvement of customer satisfaction. Companies should also assess the potential impact of AI initiatives on their competitiveness and market position.

1.3 Measuring And Evaluating Ai Success

Measuring and evaluating the success of AI initiatives is essential to ensure that AI investments produce the expected results. Businesses need to monitor KPIs, analyze AI model performance, and collect user feedback to assess the impact of AI on their operations.

Monitoring KPIs: Companies should regularly monitor the KPIs defined in the AI roadmap. This helps track progress and identify areas requiring adjustment. For example, if a KPI is to reduce operational costs, businesses should track savings from automation and compare those results to set goals.

Performance Analysis of AI Models: The performance of AI models should be evaluated in terms of accuracy, speed and robustness. Companies should use validation data sets to test models and ensure they generalize well to new data. Metrics such as precision, recall, and F1-score can be used to evaluate the performance of models.

User Feedback: It is important to collect feedback from end users to assess the impact of AI on their daily tasks and their satisfaction. Businesses can use surveys, interviews, and focus groups to gain insights into user experience and identify possible improvements. For example, if a chatbot is used for customer service, user feedback may reveal problems with understanding or relevance of responses.

Adjusting Strategies: Based on KPIs, model performance and user feedback, companies should be prepared to adjust their AI strategies. This may include updating models, adjusting operational processes, or revising objectives. Continuous improvement is essential to fully realize the benefits of AI and to adapt to market and technological developments.

1.4 Continuous Adaptation And Innovation

AI is an ever-evolving field, and businesses must be prepared to continually adapt and innovate. This includes exploring new technologies, updating employee skills, and regularly reevaluating AI strategies.

Exploring New Technologies: Businesses need to stay informed about the latest advances in AI and explore new technologies that could improve their operations. This may include emerging technologies such as deep learning, cognitive AI and explainable AI. Companies can participate in conferences, webinars and research groups to stay at the forefront of AI innovation.

Updating Skills: Employee skills must be regularly updated to keep pace with technological developments. Companies should invest in training and professional development programs to improve the AI skills of their employees. For example, training on machine learning algorithms, natural language processing (NLP) techniques, and data analysis tools may be offered.

Reevaluation of Strategies: AI strategies should be reevaluated regularly to ensure they remain aligned with business goals and priorities. Companies must be flexible and ready to adjust their strategies based on market changes, technological advances and user feedback. For example, a company may decide to explore new applications of AI if it identifies promising market opportunities or technological innovations.

Culture of Innovation and Experimentation: Companies must foster a culture of innovation and experimentation, encouraging teams to test new ideas and learn from failures. This may include setting up innovation labs, mentoring programs and internal competitions to stimulate creativity and innovation. A culture of innovation allows businesses to remain competitive and take advantage of the opportunities offered by advances in AI.

In conclusion, developing an AI strategy for your business requires careful planning, rigorous assessment of needs and opportunities, and a commitment to continuous improvement and innovation. By developing a clear roadmap, defining strategic objectives aligned with business priorities, regularly measuring and evaluating the success of AI initiatives, and adapting to technological developments, companies can maximize benefits of AI and maintain their competitiveness in the market.

CHAPTER 2: ETHICS AND REGULATION OF AI

2.1 Ethical Considerations For Using Ai

The use of AI raises important ethical questions, such as data privacy, transparency of algorithms, and the impact of automated decisions on individuals. Companies must adopt ethical practices to ensure their AI systems respect user rights and minimize bias and discrimination.

Data Privacy: Data privacy is one of the main ethical concerns related to AI. Businesses must ensure that the data collected is protected from unauthorized access and used responsibly. For example, users' personal information must be anonymized or pseudonymized to protect their identity. Companies must also obtain explicit consent from users before collecting and using their data.

Algorithm Transparency: Algorithm transparency is essential to guarantee the trust of users and regulators. Companies need to be clear about how their algorithms work, the types of data used, and the decision-making processes. For example, companies can publish technical documents and audit reports to explain AI models and their impacts. Transparency also allows users to understand how their data is used and challenge automated decisions if necessary.

Impact of Automated Decisions: Automated decisions made by AI systems can have significant consequences on individuals. For example, credit algorithms can affect people's access to loans, and recruitment systems can influence job opportunities. Companies must ensure that their AI systems make fair and equitable decisions, minimizing bias and avoiding discrimination. This may include rigorous testing and regular audits to assess model performance and fairness.

Challenge Mechanisms: Companies must provide mechanisms for users to challenge automated decisions. For example, a candidate rejected by an automated recruiting system should have the option to request a manual review of their application. These protest mechanisms allow users to defend their rights and ensure greater accountability for AI systems.

2.2 Transparency And Accountability

Transparency and accountability are essential to ensure user and regulator trust in AI systems. Companies must document and audit AI models, explain the decisions made by the algorithms, and establish governance processes to oversee the use of AI.

Documentation and Audit: Companies must document the development, training and deployment processes of AI models. This includes data collection and preparation, choice of algorithms, validation methods and test results. Regular audits must be carried out to verify compliance with current standards and regulations. For example, an audit can check whether the data used is representative and whether the algorithms are free of bias.

Explanation of Decisions: Companies must be able to explain the decisions made by their

AI algorithms. This is particularly important for systems that have a significant impact on individuals, such as credit, recruitment or medical diagnostic systems. Explainable AI approaches aim to make algorithm decisions more understandable for users and regulators. For example, techniques like white-box models and visualizations of decision factors can help explain how and why a decision was made.

AI Governance : Companies need to have governance processes in place to oversee the use of AI. This may include establishing ethics committees, designating compliance officers, and developing internal policies to guide the development and deployment of AI systems. AI governance helps ensure that company practices are aligned with ethical principles and applicable regulations.

Fairness and Non-Discrimination: Responsibility also involves ensuring that AI models are fair and non-discriminatory. Companies must assess and mitigate bias in data and algorithms, and continually monitor model performance to detect and correct potential biases. For example, bias detection and correction techniques can be integrated into the model development process to ensure that they treat all users fairly.

2.3 Ai Regulations And Standards

AI regulations vary from country to country, but generally aim to protect users' rights and ensure the ethical use of AI. Businesses must comply with applicable laws and regulations, such as GDPR in Europe, which imposes strict data protection and transparency requirements.

General Data Protection Regulation (GDPR): The GDPR imposes strict obligations on companies that collect, process and store personal data of EU residents. Companies must obtain explicit consent from users, guarantee the right to access, rectification and deletion of data, and notify data breaches. For example, a company using AI for market analysis must ensure that any personal data used is processed in accordance with GDPR requirements.

California Consumer Privacy Act (CCPA): In the United States, the CCPA provides California residents with similar data protection rights.

Companies must inform consumers of the data collected, allow access and deletion of the data, and provide the opportunity to opt out of the sale of their data. Companies must adapt their practices to comply with CCPA requirements, particularly when using personal data in their AI systems.

Industry Standards: Organizations like the Institute of Electrical and Electronics Engineers (IEEE) and the International Organization for Standardization (ISO) are developing standards to guide the ethical and responsible development and deployment of AI. For example, the IEEE has published guidelines on the ethical design of AI systems, while the ISO is working on standards for risk assessment and quality management of algorithms. Companies can refer to these standards to align their practices with industry best practices.

2.4 Future Ethical Challenges

Rapid advances in AI pose new ethical challenges that require continued reflection and action. For example, the use of AI in facial recognition and surveillance raises privacy and civil liberties concerns.

Facial Recognition and Surveillance: AI used for facial recognition and surveillance poses significant risks to privacy and civil liberties. For example, the use of surveillance cameras with facial recognition capabilities can enable mass surveillance without consent of individuals. Businesses and governments must ensure that these technologies are used responsibly and respect the rights of individuals. Strict regulations and transparency controls can help mitigate these risks.

Ethics of Machine Learning Algorithms: Machine learning algorithms can reproduce or amplify existing biases in the data, leading to discriminatory decisions. For example, a recruiting algorithm trained on historical data may discriminate against candidates from certain demographic groups if it learns about biased recruiting practices. Companies must develop fair algorithms and include mechanisms to detect and correct bias.

Societal Impacts of AI: Advances in AI can also have broader societal impacts, such as work automation and economic inequality. For example, the automation of repetitive tasks can lead to the elimination of some jobs, affecting low-skilled workers. Businesses should consider these impacts and explore solutions to mitigate negative effects, such as training and developing new skills for affected workers.

Participation in Industry Discussions and Initiatives: Companies must stay informed of developments in AI regulation and ethics, participate in industry discussions and initiatives, and commit to ethical practices and responsible. This includes participating in AI ethics working groups, conferences, and forums. By collaborating with other industry players, companies can contribute to the development of ethical standards and regulations that ensure the responsible use of AI.

In conclusion, the ethics and regulation of AI are crucial aspects to ensure responsible and equitable use of this technology. Companies must adopt ethical practices, ensure transparency and accountability, comply with current regulations, and anticipate future ethical challenges to maximize the benefits of AI while minimizing the risks to individuals and society.

CHAPTER 3: PREPARING YOUR BUSINESS FOR THE FUTURE OF AI

3.1 Emerging Trends In Ai

Emerging trends in AI include advances in natural language processing (NLP), computer vision, reinforcement learning, and generative AI. These technologies open up new possibilities for businesses, such as automating creative processes, improving human-machine interaction and developing more adaptive intelligent systems.

Natural Language Processing (NLP): NLP continues to advance, allowing machines to understand and generate human language in a more natural and contextual way. For example, text generation models, like GPT-4, can produce high-quality content, write emails or even write articles. Businesses can use NLP to improve customer support with smarter chatbots, automate document writing, or analyze sentiment in customer reviews.

Computer Vision: Computer vision allows machines to understand and interpret images and videos. Advances in this area enable applications such as facial recognition, automated visual inspection and autonomous driving. For example, manufacturing companies can use computer vision to detect defects on production lines, while retailers can use it to improve the in-store customer experience with contactless payment systems.

Reinforcement Learning: Reinforcement learning is a technique where algorithms learn to make decisions by receiving rewards or punishments for their actions. This method is used in fields such as robotics, video games and energy management. Businesses can leverage reinforcement learning to optimize complex processes, such as inventory management, production planning, or supply chain optimization.

Generative AI: Generative AI uses neural networks to create new content, such as images, videos or music. For example, GANs (Generative Adversarial Networks) can generate realistic images from textual descriptions. Businesses can use generative AI to develop creative products, such as personalized designs, innovative advertising campaigns or engaging multimedia content.

Businesses should monitor these trends and assess their potential to improve operations and offer innovative new products and services.

3.2 Impact Of New Technologies On Ai

New technologies, such as 5G, quantum computing, and advanced IoT sensors, are having a significant impact on AI by increasing processing capacity, improving connectivity, and providing richer, more accurate data.

5G: 5G offers much faster connection speeds and reduced latency, allowing AI systems to process real-time data with great efficiency. For example, autonomous vehicles can use 5G to communicate with each other and with road infrastructure, improving traffic safety and efficiency. Businesses can also use 5G to deploy advanced IoT solutions in industrial environments, such as smart factories and connected cities.

Quantum Computing: Quantum computing promises to revolutionize AI by solving complex problems much faster than classical computers. For example, quantum algorithms can optimize investment portfolios, simulate molecules for drug discovery, or solve complex logistics problems. Companies must prepare to exploit these advances by investing in research and collaborating with quantum computing research institutes.

Advanced IoT Sensors: Advanced IoT sensors provide more accurate, real-time data, enabling AI systems to make more informed decisions. For example, sensors in smart buildings can monitor energy usage, environmental conditions, and occupant behaviors to optimize resource management. Businesses can use this data to improve operational efficiency, reduce costs and offer personalized services.

Businesses must prepare to exploit these emerging technologies to remain competitive and innovative.

3.3 Training And Skills Development In Ai

AI training and skills development are essential to prepare employees to work with new technologies. Companies should offer continuing education programs, workshops, and certifications in AI to ensure their teams have the necessary skills.

Continuing Education Programs: Companies must invest in continuing education programs to keep their employees' skills up to date. This may include online courses, hands-on workshops and corporate training sessions. For example, platforms like Coursera, edX and Udacity offer specialized courses in AI and machine learning, which employees can take to improve their skills.

AI Certifications: Obtaining AI certifications can help employees demonstrate their expertise and advance in their careers. Companies can encourage their employees to earn recognized certifications, such as the TensorFlow Developer, AWS Certified Machine Learning, and Microsoft Certified: Azure AI Engineer certifications. These certifications cover key skills in AI model development, AI solution deployment, and AI project management.

Collaboration with Universities and Research Institutes: Companies can collaborate with universities and research institutes to access the latest knowledge and best practices in AI. For example, they can sponsor research programs, participate in collaborative projects or offer internships to AI students. This collaboration allows companies to stay at the forefront of innovation and benefit from academic expertise.

3.4 Building A Culture Of Innovation

To take full advantage of AI, businesses must create a culture of innovation that encourages creativity, experimentation and risk-taking. This involves promoting a growth mindset, recognizing and rewarding innovative contributions, and providing a collaborative and stimulating work environment.

Promote a Growth Mindset: Companies must encourage a growth mindset by inspiring employees to learn new skills, take on challenges and adapt to changes. This may include mentoring programs, personal development workshops and continuing education opportunities. By fostering a growth mindset, companies can help their employees thrive and innovate.

Recognize and Reward Innovative Contributions: Companies should recognize and reward employees who come up with innovative ideas and contribute to the success of AI projects. This may include bonuses, promotions, public recognition and professional development opportunities. By valuing innovative contributions, companies encourage a culture of innovation and motivate their employees to innovate.

Collaborative and Stimulating Work Environment: Companies must create a collaborative and stimulating work environment that promotes innovation. This may include open workspaces, online collaboration tools and flexible working practices. For example, innovation labs and co-working spaces can allow teams to work together on AI projects and explore new ideas.

Innovation Management Practices: Companies can adopt innovation management practices to encourage creativity and experimentation. This can include organizing hackathons, innovation competitions and incubation programs to explore new ideas and technologies. Partnerships with startups and technology companies can also provide opportunities for collaborative innovation.

In conclusion, preparing your business for the future of AI requires monitoring emerging trends, leveraging new technologies, training and upskilling employees, and building a culture of innovation. By adopting these strategies, businesses can take full advantage of the opportunities offered by AI and remain competitive in an ever-changing technology landscape.

CHAPTER 4: CASE STUDIES AND FUTURE PERSPECTIVES

4.1 Case Studies Of Innovative Companies In Ai

Case studies of innovative AI companies offer real-world examples of how AI can transform operations and create value.

Here are some notable examples:

Google: Google uses AI to improve its search engines and advertising services. Using machine learning algorithms, Google can provide more relevant search results and personalize ads based on user behaviors and preferences. For example, Google's RankBrain system uses deep learning to interpret search queries and provide more accurate results. In advertising, Google Ads uses AI to optimize bids and target ads, increasing ROI for advertisers.

Tesla: Tesla integrates AI into its autonomous vehicles to provide safe and intelligent driving experiences. Tesla's self-driving systems use neural networks to analyze sensor data in real time, recognize objects, predict the movements of surrounding vehicles and make driving decisions. For example, Tesla's Autopilot system can change lanes, adjust speed and park autonomously. These AI capabilities improve safety, reduce driver fatigue, and pave the way for broader adoption of autonomous vehicles.

Amazon : Amazon uses AI to optimize its logistics operations and improve the customer experience. Amazon's AI algorithms handle demand forecasting, inventory optimization, and delivery scheduling. For example, Amazon's warehouse management system uses intelligent robots to move products efficiently, reducing processing times and operational costs. Additionally, Amazon's recommendation systems use collaborative filtering techniques to suggest relevant products to customers, thereby increasing sales and customer satisfaction.

IBM Watson: IBM Watson helps healthcare professionals diagnose and treat complex diseases by analyzing large sets of medical data. Watson can identify possible treatment options, evaluate their effectiveness, and recommend personalized protocols for patients. For example, Watson for Oncology helps oncologists develop treatment plans based on the latest clinical data and medical research. This use of AI improves patient care and reduces medical errors.

Each case study highlights the challenges faced, solutions implemented and results achieved, providing valuable insights for businesses looking to adopt AI.

4.2 Lessons Learned And Best Practices

Lessons learned from companies that have successfully integrated AI can guide other companies on their own journeys. Here are some best practices:

Data Collection and Management: Data quality is crucial to the success of AI projects. Businesses must invest in robust data infrastructures and put data management processes in place to ensure data is clean, complete and relevant. For example, companies should implement data governance policies, use data integration tools, and conduct regular audits to ensure data quality.

Development and Deployment of AI Models: Developing AI models requires expertise in data science and software engineering. Companies must train and hire qualified talent, use proven machine learning frameworks, and adopt agile development practices to quickly iterate and improve models. For example, using development platforms like TensorFlow or PyTorch can accelerate model development, while DevOps methodologies can facilitate continuous deployment and release management.

Managing Ethical and Regulatory Challenges: Companies must adopt ethical practices to ensure that their AI systems respect user rights and minimize bias and discrimination. This includes transparency on the use of AI, the establishment of challenge mechanisms for automated decisions, and compliance with current regulations such as the GDPR. Companies should also continually monitor model performance to detect and correct potential biases.

Learning and Adaptation: AI is a constantly evolving field, and companies must be ready to learn from their failures and adjust their strategies based on the feedback and results obtained. For example, companies can use iterative feedback cycles to improve models, hold continuing education sessions for employees, and participate in communities of practice to share knowledge and experiences.

4.3 Future Perspectives For Ai In Business

The future outlook for AI in business is bright, with continued advances in technologies and increasingly sophisticated applications. Here are some key areas where AI could have a major impact:

Intelligent Automation: AI will continue to automate increasingly complex tasks, freeing up employees to focus on higher value tasks. For example, robotic process automation (RPA) systems can be enhanced by AI to manage complex workflows and make real-time decisions.

Personalized Customer Experience: AI will enable businesses to further personalize the customer experience by analyzing customer behaviors and preferences. For example, e-commerce platforms can use AI to offer hyper-personalized product recommendations, while streaming services can personalize content based on individual tastes.

Operations Optimization: AI can optimize operations in real-time using IoT sensor data and predictive analytics. For example, manufacturing companies can use AI to predict equipment failures and plan proactive maintenance, thereby reducing downtime and maintenance costs.

Product and Service Innovation: AI will open up new opportunities for product and service innovation. For example, companies can use generative AI to design new products, test them virtually, and optimize their performance before production. Additionally, intelligent services, such as virtual assistants and advanced chatbots, will improve customer interaction and increase satisfaction.

Businesses that proactively and strategically adopt AI will be better positioned to take advantage of the opportunities presented by this technology and remain competitive in a rapidly changing environment.

4.4 Conclusions And Recommendations

In conclusion, integrating AI into businesses offers significant benefits in terms of efficiency, innovation and competitiveness. To succeed in this new era of AI, businesses must:

Develop Clear Strategies: Develop AI strategies aligned with business objectives and define detailed action plans for implementation.

Invest in Skills and Technologies: Train employees in AI skills, recruit specialized talent and invest in the necessary technological infrastructure.

Adopt Ethical and Responsible Practices: Guarantee the transparency, accountability and fairness of AI systems, and comply with current regulations.

Continuously Evaluate Needs and Performance: Use KPIs to monitor progress, analyze model performance and adjust strategies based on the results obtained.

Adapt to Emerging Trends: Monitor technology trends and be ready to adopt new technologies and methods to stay competitive.

Foster a Culture of Innovation: Encourage creativity, experimentation and risk-taking, and create a collaborative and stimulating work environment.

By adopting these recommendations, businesses can maximize the benefits of AI and prepare for a future where AI plays a central role in business operations and innovation.

CONCLUSION

The potential of artificial intelligence to transform businesses is immense. By taking a strategic approach and investing in the right technologies and skills, businesses can not only improve their current operations, but also prepare for a future marked by innovation and competitiveness. This book provided a comprehensive guide to understanding, integrating and leveraging AI in business. Businesses must now take action, applying insights and recommendations to succeed in this new technological era.

Summary Of Key Points

1. Understand AI: Businesses must first understand the fundamental concepts of AI, including its different branches like natural language processing, computer vision, and reinforcement learning. An in-depth knowledge of these areas makes it possible to better identify application opportunities in the company.

2. Developing AI Strategies: A well-defined AI strategy, aligned with overall business goals, is crucial. This includes developing a roadmap, identifying strategic objectives, and establishing mechanisms to measure and evaluate the success of AI initiatives.

3. Integration and Optimization: Integrating AI into business operations requires rigorous data management, development and deployment of effective models, and automation of business processes to improve efficiency and uptake. decision.

4. Ethics and Regulation: Companies must adopt ethical practices, ensure transparency and accountability, and comply with applicable regulations to ensure fair and responsible use of AI.

5. Preparing for the Future: Preparing for the future of AI involves monitoring emerging trends, leveraging new technologies, training and upskilling employees, and creating a culture of innovation within of the company.

Call To Action

Businesses now have the tools and knowledge to transform their operations with AI. It's time to take action:

- Initial Assessment: Start by assessing your current AI maturity and identify priority areas where AI can have the greatest impact.

- Training and Awareness: Invest in the ongoing training of your employees so that they acquire the necessary skills in AI.

- Pilot Development : Launch pilot projects to test specific applications of AI in your business, measuring results and adjusting strategies based on learnings.

- Continuous Evaluation: Regularly monitor the performance and impact of the AI solutions implemented, using clear KPIs and collecting feedback to continuously improve.

By taking these steps, businesses can not only reap the immediate benefits of AI, but also position themselves as leaders in adopting advanced technologies, ready to seize the opportunities of tomorrow. The journey to an AI-powered business begins now.

LEXICON

Algorithm

A set of specific rules or instructions for solving a problem or carrying out a task. In AI, algorithms are used to create models that can make decisions based on data.

Machine Learning

A subfield of artificial intelligence where computers use algorithms to analyze data, learn from it, and make predictions or decisions without being explicitly programmed for each task.

Deep Learning

A branch of machine learning that uses multi-layered artificial neural networks to model complex data. It is particularly effective for tasks like image recognition and natural language processing.

Supervised Learning

A type of machine learning where the model is

trained on labeled data, that is, datasets where inputs are matched with correct outputs. The model learns from these examples to make predictions on new data.

Unsupervised Learning

A type of machine learning where the model analyzes unlabeled data to discover hidden structures or patterns. Common techniques include clustering and principal component analysis.

Reinforcement Learning

A machine learning technique where an agent learns to make decisions by interacting with an environment and receiving rewards or punishments for its actions. Used in areas like robotics and gaming.

Big Data

Extremely large and complex data sets that require advanced technologies and techniques for their storage, management and analysis. AI often uses big data to train and improve its models.

Clustering

An unsupervised learning technique used to group similar objects into clusters or groups. Used for market segmentation, customer classification, etc.

Anomaly Detection

Identifying data or behaviors that deviate from the norm. Used for fraud detection, predictive maintenance, etc.

Collaborative Filtering

A recommendation technique that predicts a user's interests by analyzing the preferences of similar users. Used by platforms like Netflix and Amazon.

Internet of Things (IoT)

A network of physical objects equipped with sensors, software, and other technologies to exchange data with other devices and systems over the Internet. AI can analyze IoT data for applications like smart homes and connected factories.

Quantum Computing

An emerging field of computer science that uses the principles of quantum mechanics to perform calculations much faster than classical computers for certain types of problems.

Key Performance Indicators (KPIs)

Quantifiable measures used to evaluate the success of a specific organization, project, or activity. In the context of AI, KPIs can include model accuracy, ROI, etc.

Artificial Intelligence (AI)

The simulation of human intelligence processes by machines, in particular computer systems. These processes include learning, reasoning, and self-correction.

Natural Language Processing (NLP)

Natural language processing is a branch of AI that focuses on the interaction between computers and humans using natural language. NLP allows machines to understand, interpret and respond to human language.

Artificial Neural Network

Computational models inspired by the human brain, composed of layers of artificial neurons. Used in deep learning to model complex data.

GDPR (General Data Protection Regulation)

European data protection and privacy regulations for all individuals within the EU and the European Economic Area. It imposes strict obligations on companies that collect and process personal data.

Robo-advisor

An automated financial advisor that provides investment advice and manages portfolios using AI-powered algorithms. Used to make financial services more accessible and less expensive.

Natural Language Processing (NLP)

A sub-discipline of AI that allows machines to understand, interpret and generate human language. Used in applications like chatbots, machine translation and sentiment analysis.

Computer Vision

A field of AI that allows computers to understand and interpret images and videos. Used in applications such as facial recognition, medical image analysis and autonomous driving.

www.ingramcontent.com/pod-product-compliance
Lightning Source LLC
Chambersburg PA
CBHW050100230526
45470CB00004B/1619